"If you feel you could use some help growing closer to Mary, I can think of no better guide than Fr. John Riccardo. Instead of assuming you already have it all figured out, his writing meets you where you are and helps break down the barriers that keep you from a life-giving relationship with her. *Learning to Trust from Mary: Meditations on the Rosary* will help you encounter Mary in a life-changing way. The Blessed Mother is more than a great example to follow. She lives to pray for us, intercede for us, and fight for us. This book will help you see how you can personally experience Mary as your mother and advocate."

Lisa Brenninkmeyer
Founder, Walking with Purpose

"Whether you are new to a relationship with Mary, or have been blessed by the goodness of God's Mother for a long time, this little book is packed with faith, and hope, and love. I urge everyone to read these words of Fr. John Riccardo. This is an especially important text in today's tumultuous world. Let all of us ask the Blessed Mother for help in these times!"

Sister Ann Shields
Servants of God's Love,
Radio Evangelist: *Food for the Journey*

Learning to Trust from Mary

Meditations on the Rosary

Fr. John Riccardo

Illustrated by Marie Mattos

Learning to Trust from Mary:
Meditations on the Rosary

Scripture quotations are from the Revised Standard Version of the Bible—Second
Catholic Edition (Ignatius Edition), copyright © 2006
National Council of the Churches of Christ in the United States of America.
Used by permission. All rights reserved.

Layout and Cover Design by Jacqueline L. Challiss Hill

Illustrations by Marie Mattos

ISBN: 978-1-7364920-1-7
eISBN: 978-1-7364920-2-4
Library of Congress Control Number: 2021945869

Printed in the United States

ACTS XXIX Press
1050 Porter St., Detroit, MI 48226
actsxxix.org | press@actsxxix.org

The Word Among Us Press
7115 Guilford Dr., Ste. 100, Frederick, MD 21704
wau.org

Table of Contents

Introduction

In October 2010, I had the opportunity to travel to Poland on a pilgrimage with a number of people. One of the many highlights for me was the celebration of Mass at the Shrine of Our Lady of Czestochowa, one of the most significant Marian shrines in the world and a true spiritual center for the Polish people. To help me prayerfully prepare for the pilgrimage, I had printed out the various homilies and addresses that Pope John Paul II had given during his very first trip to Poland right after he had been elected Pope in 1978. I was profoundly struck by something that he said while he was at the Shrine of Our Lady of Czestochowa just before he consecrated Poland again to her care. He said simply this: "I am a man of great trust. I learnt to be so here."[1]

As many of us probably know, Pope John Paul II said over and over again, "Do not be afraid." In fact, these were among the very first words he said to the world as Pope that evening from the balcony at St. Peter's Basilica after he was announced to the world as the newest successor of the man buried beneath that basilica. But how in the world could it be that this man, whose mother died as a very young child, who shortly thereafter lost his brother and then his father, and who endured the oppression of two of the fiercest and most brutal totalitarian regimes in world history, could be a man of such confidence, of such trust, and of such hope?

It seemed that here, during his return to the Shrine of Our Lady of Czestochowa, he was giving us a clue to the answer. It seemed as though he was saying that it was at the feet of Mary, at the school of Mary, if you will, that he learned to be a man of great trust. In other words, Mary taught him how to trust. In saying this to us, he seemed to be begging us also to sit at the feet of this woman chosen by God to be the mother of His Son. He seemed to be begging us to see that Mary is not some statue that stands in our churches but a real person, living now with the Lord in heaven and a person who had to grow in trust herself. Because no human person ever knew Jesus like she did, she was and is uniquely qualified to teach us how to trust.

I think we can forget sometimes that Mary had to learn to trust herself. But clearly, she did. She certainly had to learn to trust that the message Gabriel delivered to her would in fact come true, namely, that she would conceive in her womb a child without the aid of a man.

She had to trust that God would somehow, *somehow*, help her husband, Joseph, to whom she had already been married but with whom she had not yet lived, to believe against all odds that the child in her womb was not the result of infidelity on her part but was really the result of God's action in her.

She had to learn to trust that God would give her the strength to endure the gossip and the stares of her many nosy neighbors in that small village of Nazareth where surely people talked about her unique situation.

She had to learn to trust that God would provide for her and her child when Herod went on a warpath seeking to kill all the children in the area where she was living.

She had to learn to trust that God would provide a job for her husband when they fled to Egypt though they might not have had any connections there or have even spoken the language.

She had to trust that God would provide for her when Joseph died, an event that surely had happened although we know nothing about it or else it would have been absurd for Jesus to have given Mary over to the protection of the apostle John from the Cross.

She had to learn to trust that all she had gone through was somehow going to amount to something when Jesus, whom she *knew* was no mere man, was still at home at the age of twenty, twenty-five, twenty-nine, making who knows what in His carpenter shop.

She had to learn to trust when she heard and saw the rejection of the townspeople to her son, even going so far as to call Him the devil.

She had to learn to trust when He was arrested, betrayed by one of His best friends, a man she knew.

She had to learn to trust when her son was

being tortured nearly to death.

She had to learn to trust when she saw Him on the way to Calvary, carrying a cross, unjustly condemned to death.

She had to learn to trust when she was standing beneath His Cross, when His precious blood was pouring out of His head crowned with thorns, and His hands and feet, which had been punctured by nails the size of small railroad ties.

She had to learn to trust when she saw and heard Him breathe His last breath.

She had to learn to trust when He was taken down from the Cross and placed in her arms, even as she once held Him in her arms when He was a child.

She had to learn to trust when He was wrapped in a burial shroud and placed in a tomb.

She had to learn to trust when she tried to go to bed on that first agonizing night after He had died, not knowing that anything further was coming.

She had to learn to trust when she tried to go about her day on that Saturday that we now call "Holy."

She had to learn to trust when she woke up the first day of the week, a day not yet known as Easter.

Yes, Mary had to learn to trust.

And because no one had to learn it more than she, and because no one saw God's faithfulness more than she, she is able to teach us to trust like no one else can. For this reason, the Rosary can be a great school and a kind of classroom with Mary as our instructor helping us to know her son in a way that only a mother can. This should be our aim as we pray the various Mysteries of the Rosary. Rather than just merely mouthing words, we should gaze at the various events of the life of Jesus asking the intercession of the woman who knew Him best and who knows Him best, that they may not be mere events of history for us but events that happened *for* us out of God's great love and mercy so that we may have the fullness of life.

Now, having said all of this, mine has been a very slow and at times difficult journey to the Rosary, to be honest, and one that is certainly by no means finished. Because I know so many people who find either the basic practice of asking the prayers of the saints in general or praying the Rosary in particular to be hard to understand, I thought a few observations might be helpful.

Let me then offer some general remarks about the intercession of the saints, move on to some personal reflections about Mary, and then conclude with some, hopefully, helpful comments about this simple yet profound and powerful prayer.

First, some basic thoughts about the intercession of the saints.

The key question, it seems to me, is whether or not the saints are dead. The answer to that, of course, is a resounding NO! In responding to the testing of the Sadducees in the gospel, that is that group of men who denied that there was a resurrection, Jesus referred them to the passage in the Book of Exodus when God reveals His name to Moses and told Moses that He is "the God of Abraham, the God of Isaac, and the God of Jacob" (Exo. 3:6) even though these men had all died many years before. In answering this way, Jesus means to explain God is revealing to Moses, and us, that these men are alive, not dead, even though they left this earth long ago. And so God *is*, not *was*, the God of Abraham, Isaac, and Jacob.

St. Paul, in his letter to the Philippians, writes, "For me to live is Christ, and to die is gain" (Phil. 1:21). "I am hard pressed between the two," he says. "My desire is to depart and to be with Christ" (Phil. 1:23). Clearly death for Paul is not an end, not an end at all. It's rather the doorway by which we go home to be with the Lord. Paul's hope, our hope, comes directly from the mouth of Jesus, who said to Martha when He arrived at her brother Lazarus's tomb, "I am the resurrection and the life; he who believes in me, though he die, yet shall he live" (John 11:25). Because of the resurrection of Jesus, death is not the end, it does not have the last word. The last word belongs to God. The God who is love, whose love is truly stronger than death. And the last word is life.

The saints, then, those that have gone before us marked with the sign of faith, are not dead. But because they are not dead, there is still a very real fellowship with them. This, I think, is what often causes confusion for many people. Sometimes this arises when people say that they "pray" to the saints, which sounds very much like something that should only be done to God. And if by "pray," a person means "worship," then they're right; that is something that should only be done to God. We are to worship God and God alone. But if "pray" is used here more or less synonymously with "talked to," which I think it is for most people, then there's nothing at all objectionable to this. Why? Well, because we believe in the communion of Saints. We say this every Sunday in The Creed. This communion includes not only those here below but those who are already with the Lord in glory, as well as those that are on their way home through purgation. It is, as is often said, a very thin veil between us and them. Death does not end our friendships or our communion, however much it may change, and it does change, the manner in which we can be experienced or we can experience them.

About this very real communion of Saints, Saint Thérèse of Lisieux once wrote, "I promise to have you taste after my departure for eternal life the happiness one can find in feeling a friendly soul next to oneself."[2]

To these realities that the saints are not dead, and that we still share a fellowship, a communion, a friendship with them, we must also add this simple but important remark: it is most appropriate that we honor the saints. This is not at all strange and we do it all the time here on earth. For example, we honor great statesmen and women, great athletes, great actors and actresses, and above all men and women in our families who left enduring marks in our lives. To do this in no way detracts from the God who made these men and women; it rather serves to highlight His artistry for it is God who creates us all. This is in large part why we have pictures in our homes of loved ones who have died. We don't worship the pictures; we have them up as tangible reminders of the people that we love and that we miss, with the aspiration, perhaps, to imitate them in our own lives.

How much more is this appropriate for the saints, those truly great men and women in life, the members of what I often think of God's Hall of Fame, the only one, really, that ultimately matters?

So if the saints are not dead and if there is a real communion still between us, a next question might seem to be something like, "Well, then, what are they doing now?"

When asked by the lawyer which of the Commandments of the Law is the greatest, Jesus responded by saying, "You shall love the Lord your God with all your heart, all your soul, all your mind, and all your strength. This is the first and the greatest commandment. The second is like it. You shall love your neighbor as yourself" (cf. Matt. 22:37).

Love, we could say, is what we're made for: love of God and love of neighbor. This is not only true here but forever. In fact, much more so forever. This is the life of heaven: loving God as He deserves and as we truly want to and loving, and being loved, by each other. And the saints in heaven are doing just this: they are loving God and they are loving their neighbor. And who is their neighbor? Well, it's us!

Saint Thérèse, shortly before she died at the age of twenty-four, remarked that she was to spend her days in heaven doing good on earth.[3] In other words, the saints are not passive with regard to us. They're not sitting up there right now looking at us down here and saying to themselves, "Boy, am I glad that's over!" They're involved! They're cheering us on, helping us by their prayers.

The Letter to the Hebrews, after speaking about the many great saints in the Old Testament in chapter 11, goes on to say in chapter 12, "Therefore, since, we are surrounded by a great cloud of witnesses"—that is, the saints—"let us also lay aside every weight, and sin which clings so closely, and let us run with perseverance the race that is set before us" (12:1). The image here is of us engaged in a race in a stadium and the stands are filled beyond capacity with the saints who've gone before us, who have left us inspiring examples of true greatness. But you know as well as I do that when we go to a game as a fan, we don't go merely to watch the game. We go with the desire that somehow our cheering and our presence will help to change the outcome of the game. Just as a hundred thousand people in a football stadium often rouse eleven players to do things that on their own without the presence of the fans they could not do, so the intercession of the saints can rouse us to do great things for God.

Now, having said all of that about the saints in general, let me say a few things about Mary in particular.

If it is true that the saints are God's masterpieces—and it's true—then it must be the case that Mary is *the* masterpiece of all masterpieces. When the archangel Gabriel comes to her, he says to her not "Hail Mary," though we say that in the prayer, he says instead, "Hail, full of grace" (Luke 1:28). This is often lost in our modern translations of the Bible. The simple thing to understand here, without getting bogged down in Greek, is that Gabriel does not address Mary by her name. That is, Gabriel doesn't call her "Mary." Instead, he greets her as if her real name is this word that only shows up in this one place in the whole Bible in Greek and can be loosely understood as something like "she who is filled with grace."

Now to be clear, there is no other human person who is filled with grace. She is absolutely unique among God's creatures because no one cooperated with God's will like she did. And thus, she is deserving of our honor in a singular, remarkable way. If she did not say yes to Gabriel, or rather to God through Gabriel, we simply don't know how we would've been redeemed. But she *did* say yes. She *did* surrender herself to God entirely. And this surrender has made possible our salvation.

To sum up this notion of the saints and how honoring them is in no way inappropriate or a slight to God, let me share quickly an image I once heard. A man I know put it this way:

He said, "Imagine I was an artist—which I'm not, I assure you—and now imagine that I invited you to come over and see my showroom, filled with all sorts of incredible pieces that I had personally made from scratch. Imagine that I led you around to gaze quite intently at sculptures, paintings, etchings, and other works of art that I had fashioned. Now, I ask you: would I be offended if, as you looked at these, you said to me, 'Wow, Father, these are incredible!' Of course not!

"Well, God is the great artist and He has fashioned many incredible things. And the greatest of all these things are the saints. And the greatest of all the saints is Mary. In honoring the saints, and especially in honoring Mary, we honor the One who made them. And we don't at all take away from Him any more than recognizing my artistry—if I had any—would take away from me."

Now having said all this, I didn't always think this way. For whatever reason, I never had much of a relationship with Mary when I was growing up. I prayed all the time, but I always simply prayed to God. I didn't talk to Mary much, if at all, nor to the other saints to be honest. The start of the change for me was when I was living and studying in the seminary in Rome. There I had the great blessing of living virtually in the shadow of Pope John Paul II for four years. On many occasions I met him, and more times that I can possibly count I was in attendance for Mass, the Angelus in St. Peter's Square, or some other papal event that was taking place next door to where I lived. To listen to or to read Pope John Paul II was to know that he was intensely Marian. And not only was he intensely Marian, but he was always referring to the importance of Mary's role in the life of priests in particular, and of all the faithful in general.

You might recall that John Paul's motto as Pope was two Latin words: *totus tuus,* meaning "entirely yours." Those two words referred to his relationship to Mary. Now, this can easily be misunderstood. It was by me, in fact, for a long time. I mean if we said "entirely yours" to anybody, shouldn't that be to God? But the Pope explains this expression in a letter he wrote on the Rosary. Quoting St. Louise de Montfort, John Paul wrote, "Our entire perfection consists in being conformed, united, and consecrated to Jesus Christ. Hence, the most perfect of all devotions is undoubtedly that which conforms, unites, and consecrates us most perfectly to Jesus Christ. Now, since Mary is of all creatures the one most conformed to Jesus Christ, it follows that among all devotions that which most consecrates and conforms a soul to Our Lord is devotion to Mary, His holy mother. And that the more a soul is consecrated to her, the more it will be consecrated to Jesus Christ."[4]

Now, I'll be honest: in my case it took a very long time for these words to sink in. After hearing the Holy Father speak repeatedly about the significance of Mary, I can still remember very clearly one afternoon walking down a street in Rome leading away from St. Peter's, looking up into the sky, and praying something like this, "Jesus, I think this is somewhat backwards, but I am asking you to introduce to me your mother, please." I'll spare you all the details about how that happened, but I will simply say this for now: I have gradually come to the deep conviction that Mary is very much interested in my life and in yours. And that the Rosary is now a key part of my daily life.

Let me here make a few simple remarks

about praying the Rosary in general. If it helps at all for those who find this prayer difficult, I personally didn't begin to pray it every day until somewhat recently and I am a priest of more than twenty-five years. Although an exceptionally simple prayer, I still can find the Rosary, quite frankly, difficult and even monotonous to pray. With God's grace, though, I am now resolved to pray it every day until I die. For a variety of reasons, I have become convinced not only that am I to pray it every day, but that I am to encourage others to do the same, hence these reflections.

Why?

Well, in his letter on the Rosary in 2002, Pope John Paul II gives us one reason.

Referring back to the words of Pope Leo XIII, John Paul wrote that "the Rosary is an effective weapon against the evils afflicting society."[5] In other words, the Rosary can be a very effective way to intercede for various intentions. In that same letter, the Pope suggests two things in particular that it can be an effective weapon to pray for: one is for peace in the world and two is for families. I often gather up all the various needs that people have brought to me on a daily basis and offer the Rosary that day for those people. When you think about it, it makes sense that the Rosary would be an effective weapon against not only the various evils but ultimately against the evil one, that is, against the devil. After all, way back in the beginning when man and woman rebelled against God at the temptation of the devil, God foretold that there would be enmity between the woman and the serpent, a poetic image for the devil. In a prophetic passage in Genesis 3:15, God reveals that the seed of the woman will crush the serpent's head and that the serpent would bruise the offspring of the woman's heel. One wound, obviously, is fatal, the other is not. It was Mary's "yes" that brought about the crushing, fatal blow to the devil's head, that is, to his power, and perhaps this is the reason for his hatred, not only for Mary in particular but for women in general. The devil was undone, not by some glorious king but by the simple, obedient surrender of a poor, young peasant girl in an obscure, out-of-the-way town called Nazareth. And perhaps for this very reason, the Rosary is a very effective spiritual weapon.

So how do we pray the Rosary? Well, to put it simply there are two ways to pray it: We can either pray it quickly, in a very rote fashion and without much thinking, or we can pray it attentively. To do the latter is much easier said than done, at least it is for me. John Paul reminds us that the Rosary is what he calls an exquisitely contemplative prayer. But unless we fight to stay attentive when praying it, he goes on to say, "the Rosary is a body without a soul and its recitation runs the risk of becoming a mechanical repetition of formulas."[6]

As a means, then, to help us stay attentive throughout the praying of the Rosary, two things might be suggested. The first is what I understand is the typical way that the Germanic people pray the Rosary. This way is simply to insert the Mystery being contemplated between the two halves of the Hail Mary. So in other words, say you are praying the Sorrowful Mystery calling to mind Jesus' scourging at the pillar. The praying of the ten Hail Marys would go something like this:

Hail Mary,
full of grace,
the Lord is with thee.
Blessed art thou among women,
and blessed is the fruit of thy womb, Jesus,
who was scourged at the pillar for us.

Holy Mary,
Mother of God,
pray for us sinners now,
and at the hour of our death.

Amen.

The Pope calls this a praise-worthy custom. This can also help remind us that the Rosary is a Christological prayer, that is to say it is a reflection on what Jesus has done for us.

A second aid to staying attentive is to heed the advice of St. Ignatius of Loyola, founder of the Jesuits. Ignatius used to encourage people, whenever they prayed, to use their senses, their memory, their imagination. This is indeed a most helpful way to pray, especially when reading Scripture or praying the Rosary. In short this means that when we sit down with either the Scriptures or the various Mysteries of the Rosary, we should do everything we can to try to picture the scene, to put ourselves there or rather to ask the Holy Spirit, Who was there really and Who now lives in us really, to help us try to imagine what it sounded like in the garden when the Roman guards were crowning Jesus with thorns, what the air smelled like on that spring morning when Mary Magdalene came to Jesus' tomb, or what the face of the host at the wedding in Cana looked like when he saw and tasted a hundred and eighty gallons of water changed into wine. God gave you an imagination: use it! Goodness knows we use it for evil enough times. The solution isn't to get rid of the imagination; it's to use it for the purposes for which He gave it.

Let me conclude finally with this: what follows is not at all intended to be an exhaustive explanation of the Mysteries of the Rosary or some exhaustive commentary on Mary. Each of us has our own unique friendship with the saints in general and with Mary in particular. Your story will be very different from mine. All these are meant to be are simple reflections that hopefully can orient us to the various Mysteries that we're pondering. And I offer them with a very fervent prayer that all of us will come to know Jesus more by better reflecting on the Mysteries of His life, asking the intercession of His mother and ours. For no human being has ever known Jesus like the one who carried Him in her womb, nursed Him, and raised Him.

We as a race are always looking for heroes, for people to inspire us and to imitate. And quite frankly, there is no greater hero than Mary. And there is no better motto we can adopt for our lives than the words that Mary spoke to the archangel Gabriel on a seemingly very ordinary day when your future, my future, and the whole world's future were forever changed.

"Behold, I am the servant of the Lord. May it be done to me according to your word" (cf. Luke 1:38).

Mary's final words in Scripture are most significant. They are spoken at the wedding in Cana when they ran out of wine and she brought that need to the attention of Jesus. She said to the servants that day, "Do whatever he tells you" (John 2:5). She says the same thing to you and me right now: Do whatever He tells you.

Because Mary always points us to Jesus, may her intercession help us to hear His voice again and again, to grow in our friendship with Him and through Him by the power of His Spirit with the Father, especially as we ponder the events that saved us, and may we indeed do whatever He tells us.

How to Pray the Rosary

To pray the Rosary, follow these steps:

1. Make the Sign of the Cross and recite the Apostles' Creed.

2. Recite the Our Father.

3. Recite three Hail Marys for the virtues of Faith, Hope, and Charity.

4. Recite the Glory Be.

5. Recite the Fatima Prayer.

6. Announce the first mystery and then recite the Our Father.

7. Recite ten Hail Marys while meditating on the Mystery.

8. Recite the Glory Be.

9. Recite the Fatima Prayer.

10. Announce the next Mystery, recite the Our Father, and repeat steps 7–9 as you meditate on the remaining Mysteries.

11. Recite the Closing Prayers: Hail Holy Queen and the Final Prayer.

Traditionally, each Mystery of the Rosary is prayed on a specific day.

Monday: Joyful

Tuesday: Sorrowful

Wednesday: Glorious

Thursday: Luminous

Friday: Sorrowful

Saturday: Joyful

Sundays of Advent and Christmas: Joyful

Sundays of Lent: Sorrowful

Other Sundays: Glorious

Prayers of the Rosary

The Sign of the Cross

In the name of the Father,
and of the Son,
and of the Holy Spirit.

Amen.

Apostles' Creed

I believe in God,
the Father Almighty,
Creator of Heaven and earth,
and in Jesus Christ,
His only Son Our Lord,
Who was conceived by the Holy Spirit,
born of the Virgin Mary,
suffered under Pontius Pilate,
was crucified, died,
and was buried.

He descended into hell.
On the third day,
He rose again from the dead.

He ascended into heaven and is seated
at the right hand of God,
the Father Almighty;
from there,
He will come to judge the living
and the dead.

I believe in the Holy Spirit,
the holy Catholic Church,
the communion of saints,
the forgiveness of sins,
the resurrection of the body,
and life everlasting.

Amen.

The Our Father

Our Father,
Who art in heaven,
hallowed be Thy name.
Thy kingdom come.
Thy will be done,
on earth as it is in Heaven.
Give us this day our daily bread,
and forgive us our trespasses,
as we forgive those who trespass against us.
And lead us not into temptation,
but deliver us from evil.

Amen.

Hail Mary

Hail Mary,
full of grace,
the Lord is with thee.
Blessed art thou among women,
and blessed is the fruit of thy womb, Jesus.

Holy Mary,
Mother of God,
pray for us sinners now
and at the hour of our death.

Amen.

The Glory Be

Glory Be to the Father,
and to the Son,
and to the Holy Spirit.
As it was in the beginning,
is now,
and will be forever.

Amen.

Fatima Prayer

Oh, My Jesus,
forgive us our sins,
save us from the fires of hell,
lead all souls to heaven,
especially those in most need of Thy mercy.

Hail Holy Queen

Hail, holy Queen,
Mother of mercy,
our life, our sweetness, and our hope.

To thee do we cry,
poor banished children of Eve,
to thee do we send up our sighs, mourning,
and weeping in this valley of tears.

Turn then, most gracious advocate,
thine eyes of mercy toward us,
and after this our exile
show us the blessed fruit of thy womb, Jesus.
Oh clement, oh loving, oh sweet Virgin Mary.

Pray for us, oh Holy Mother of God.

That we may be made worthy of the
promises of Christ.

Final Prayer

Let us pray.
Oh God, whose only begotten Son,
by His life, death, and resurrection
has purchased for us the
rewards of eternal life,
grant we beseech Thee,
that while meditating upon these
Mysteries of the
most holy Rosary of the Blessed Virgin Mary,
we may imitate what they contain and obtain
what they promise,
through the same Christ our Lord.

Amen.

The Joyful Mysteries

Typically, the Church prays these Mysteries on Mondays and Saturdays. It's important to remember this simple truth as we begin the Rosary: all that we are about to contemplate was done for us, for you. God did these things for you, by name, and for me, by name. These actions of God—the virginal conception, the presentation in the temple—everything that we are about to recollect happened simply because God loves you. And love gets involved. God didn't have to do any of this. He didn't have to rescue us. He didn't have to rescue us from Sin. He didn't have to rescue us from the power of Death. He didn't have to rescue us from Hell. But He did. And so let us begin with that in mind. I *am*, you *are* the reason for all the Mysteries we are about to gaze upon.

The Sign of the Cross

Apostles' Creed

Our Father
Intention: A prayer for our Holy Father

Three Hail Marys
Intention: For an increase of faith, hope, and charity

Glory Be

The First Joyful Mystery
The Annunciation

On a real day, in a dumpy little town in the middle of nowhere quite frankly, the all-powerful God of heaven and earth, the one who created all that is seen and unseen, sent an angel to a young girl to change the history of the world forever.

This is the day the sun began to shine again. The day when God broke onto the stage that is human history by becoming flesh in the womb of that young girl.

So let us ask the Holy Spirit to bring us there now to that little house to see what Mary saw, to smell the many smells in a Middle Eastern home, to hear the voice of Gabriel speaking.

"And the virgin's name to whom he came was Mary" (cf. Luke 1:27).

Our Father

Ten Hail Marys

Glory Be

Fatima Prayer

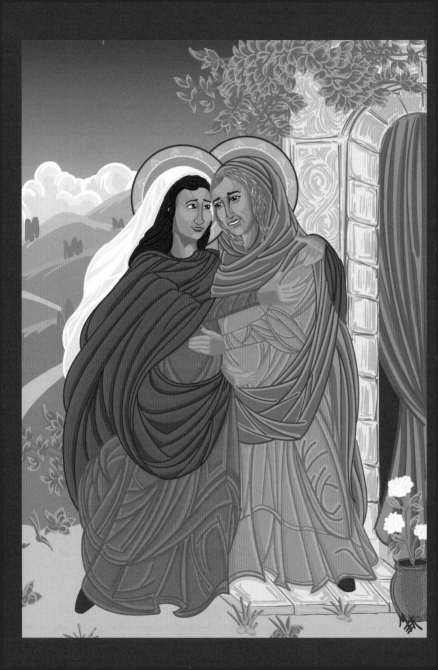

The Second Joyful Mystery
The Visitation

Mary goes to Elizabeth to make herself useful. Elizabeth is also pregnant, and so Mary goes to help her older cousin. Nothing, absolutely nothing, is impossible for God. That's the message that Gabriel had said to Mary and now she sees it with her own eyes as she looks at her cousin who she thought was past the age of bearing children. How, too, do we need to be reminded of this truth—nothing is impossible for God.

He made a virgin pregnant. He made a woman past the age of bearing children pregnant. No matter what you may be facing right now, imagine what He can and wants to do in our lives.

So let us ask these two women who experienced firsthand such miracles to pray for us that we might grow in faith.

Our Father

Ten Hail Marys

Glory Be

Fatima Prayer

The Third Joyful Mystery
The Birth of Our Lord
and Savior Jesus Christ

The King of the universe has become a tiny helpless child, placed by his mother not on a throne but in a manger. What's a manger? A manger is a trough out of which animals eat their food. The King of the universe is lying in a trough! Where? Not in Rome, the capital of the known world. Not in Athens. But in a dinky village called Bethlehem.

What's so important about Bethlehem? Bethlehem means the house of bread.

In the very first moments of His appearance in the flesh, the King of kings makes this startling point: He desires somehow unimaginably to be our food. He's already foreshadowing the great gift that is the Eucharist right at the beginning of His earthly life.

Our Father

Ten Hail Marys

Glory Be

Fatima Prayer

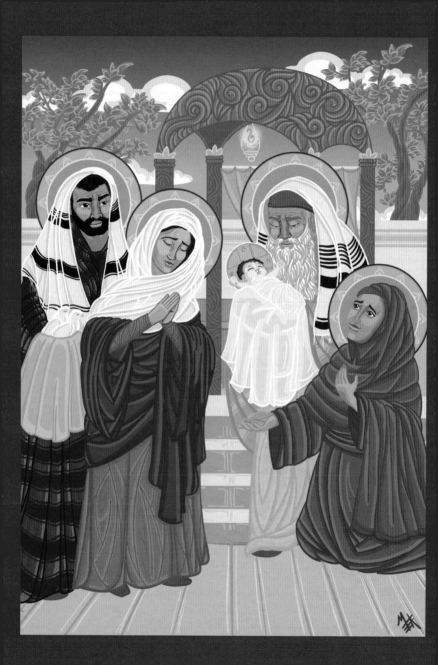

The Fourth Joyful Mystery
The Presentation in the Temple

Three different events are collected into one in this Mystery. First, the circumcision and naming of the child. Second, the purification of Mary, something that all women who had given birth underwent according to the law of Moses. And third, the ritual known as the redemption of the firstborn, a rite that's found in the Book of Numbers in chapter 18.

In the circumcision of Jesus, the covenant God had made with Abraham long ago was physically cut into Jesus' flesh and His precious blood flowed for the first time.

Immediately after this, the child was given its name by Joseph.

"Now what's in a name?" Shakespeare famously wrote once. Well, in this case, **everything** is in the name because Jesus means "God saves." This is both who He is and what He does. Whom has He come to save? He's come to save us. He's come to save you. He's come to save me.

Who could have ever hoped for something like this?

Our Father

Ten Hail Marys

Glory Be

Fatima Prayer

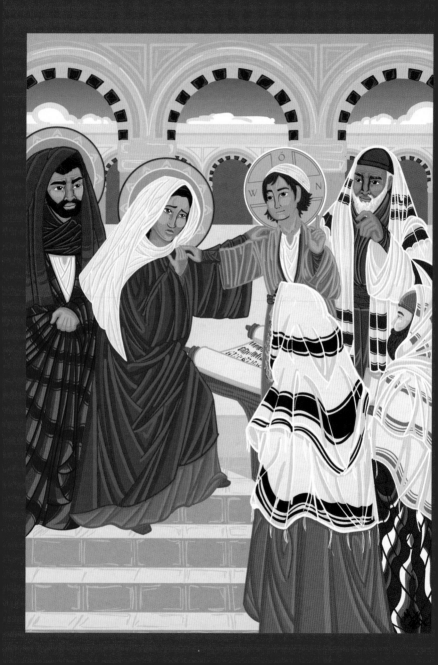

The Fifth Joyful Mystery
The Finding of the Child
Jesus in the Temple

Luke makes a point of writing that the Child Jesus, when he was twelve years old, stayed behind after the family had gone to Jerusalem to celebrate the feast of Passover.

In other words, Jesus did not get lost back in Jerusalem while the family packed up, nor did Mary and Joseph somehow forget

Him. Jesus did this very intentionally; He stayed behind.

And as He did with His mother and His foster father, Jesus often does this with us, too. He makes us search for Him. Thus, Mary's question to Him is often our question as well: why have you done this to us?

Our Father

Ten Hail Marys

Glory Be

Fatima Prayer

Hail Holy Queen

Final Prayer

The Sign of the Cross

The Sorrowful Mysteries

In these Mysteries, we beg Mary for a greater access to an understanding of all that her son suffered. This was, again and again we must remember, for us, for you, it was for me.

And yet, we cannot grasp the horror of the cross nor understand just how merciful was this willful suffering for us.

We have tragically become used to seeing a man hanging on a cross, nailed in his hands and feet. But Roman citizens were told that they should not even *look* at a crucified man; it was such a shock!

But the cross fails to shock us.

As we gaze at these Mysteries, two things seem worth asking for.

First: A greater understanding of the seriousness not just of sin but of *our* sin, of *my* sin, of *your* sin. Pope Pius XII once wrote that the most serious sin of our age was what he called a loss of "the sense of sin."[7]

A man I know, after he saw the movie *The Passion of the Christ* said "If this was the remedy for our sickness, then how great must be the sickness?"

So, in these Mysteries we also call to mind the truth that we were not saved by Jesus' teaching or by His miracles but by His Cross, that is, by His suffering. And it is important to remember that Jesus was not passive in His suffering. This was in fact *the* most active moment of His life. He was willing to be there on the Cross. You can't nail God to a cross if He doesn't want to be there. And this truth forever changes *our* sufferings. And that's the second thing we want to ask for: a deeper understanding of how God can use our own sufferings.

Now, this is not to say that suffering becomes a good thing; it does not. Suffering is never a good. But it *can* be used for good; indeed, it can be used for the *greatest* of goods.

St. Paul writes in Colossians 1:24, "I fill up in my own flesh what's lacking in the sufferings of Christ for the sake of his body which is the church." Now what in the world is lacking in the suffering of Christ? *Nothing* except for my participation in it and yours.

Jesus, to be sure, is the one and only Redeemer. But He invites you and me to share, as St. Paul makes clear, with Him in the glorious work of redeeming the world.

We do this in a most powerful way when we unite our sufferings, whatever they may be, to His on the cross for others.

As we pray these Mysteries, especially for those of us hurting in a particular way, let us trust then that our sufferings are not in vain any more than His Cross was in vain. Though you and I don't yet see how they will help to redeem the world, we need to trust that one day we will see that.

The Sign of the Cross

Apostles' Creed

Our Father
Intention: A prayer for our Holy Father

Three Hail Marys
Intention: For an increase of faith, hope, and charity

Glory Be

The First Sorrowful Mystery
The Agony in the Garden

God-made-Man is on His face in the dust, praying, sweating blood, in agony over the prospect of His impending death for you and for me.

Pope Benedict in his book *Jesus of Nazareth* writes, "He wrestled with his destiny here for my sake." In the same book, he writes about this event in the garden, saying, "because He is the Son, He sees with total clarity the whole foul flood of evil, all the power of lies and pride, all the wiles and cruelty of the evil that masks itself as life yet constantly serves to destroy, debase, and crush life. Because He is the Son, He experiences deeply all the horror, filth, and baseness. But He must drink from the chalice prepared for Him, the vast power of Sin and Death, all this He must take into Himself so that it can be disarmed and defeated in Him."[8]

Here is Christ the great athlete beginning the single most meaningful competition of all time.

So come, let us adore Him.

Our Father

Ten Hail Marys

Glory Be

Fatima Prayer

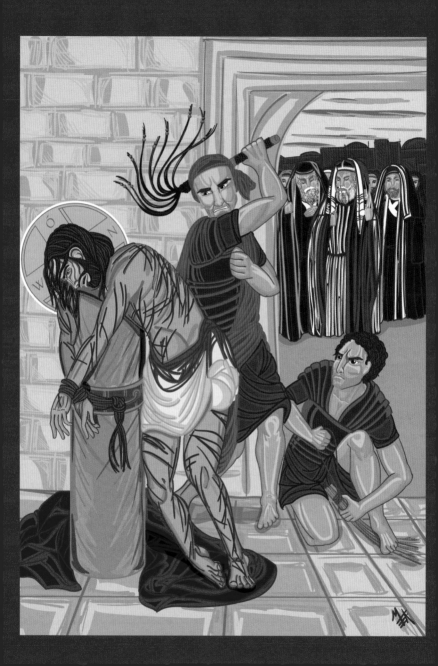

The Second Sorrowful Mystery
The Scourging at the Pillar

It goes beyond saying that this was a horrific torture. The condemned man was stripped, tied to a pillar where Roman soldiers then repeatedly beat him with whips that had little bits of iron, or bone, at the end of them until *they* got tired.

The gospel writers took for granted that this didn't need to be described. In fact, all

four of them write about this in all of one
sentence: "And Pilate had Jesus scourged"
(cf. John 19:1, Mark 15:15, Matt 27:26,
Luke 23:1). If it weren't for the graphic
nature of the scene in the movie *The
Passion of the Christ,* we might still not
understand just how brutal this was.

The most unjust court case has just
been decided and the sentencing is now
commencing. The truly innocent One, the
Good God who made all that is, is literally
being torn to shreds by the creatures that
He loves beyond all telling.

"But he was wounded," Isaiah says, *"for
our transgressions, he was bruised for our
iniquities; upon him was the chastisement*

that made us whole, and with his stripes we are healed" (Isa. 53:5).

Our Father

Ten Hail Marys

Glory Be

Fatima Prayer

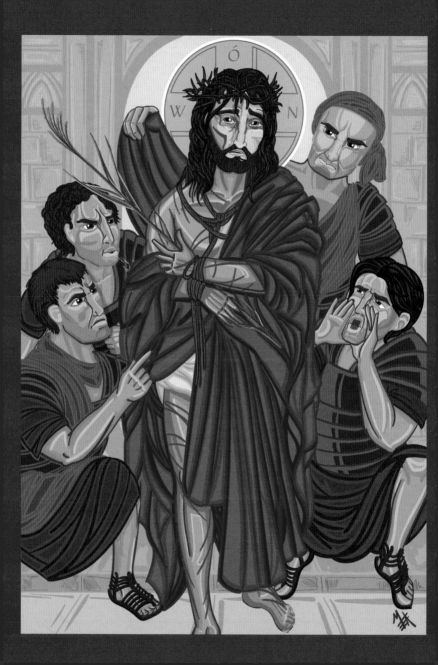

The Third Sorrowful Mystery
The Crowning with Thorns

The scourging at the pillar was not enough to sate our anger and rage against God. And so now comes a diabolical mockery of Jesus' kingship. The soldiers place a rough robe atop His already shredded skin, thrust a reed into His hands as a mock scepter, and now push a crown made out of thorns into and onto His regal head. As they do so, they bow down before Him in a mock gesture of devotion and then they beat Him with their hands.

Every time the crowds had wanted to make Jesus King in the gospels, He ran away from them for His kingship, the only real kingship, was not one of power but one of love. And only now does that kingship become clear.

A king in the Old Testament had three main responsibilities: to protect widows and orphans, to care for the poor, and to lead his people into battle, not simply to send troops out to fight but to be himself at the head of the battle.

And so, Our King alone goes now into

battle against our greatest enemies: against Sin, against Death, and against Hell.

Our Father

Ten Hail Marys

Glory Be

Fatima Prayer

The Fourth Sorrowful Mystery

The Carrying of the Cross

When Jesus appeared on the shores of the Jordan River some three years before John the Baptist had cried out "Behold, the Lamb of God, who takes away the sin of the world!" (John 1:29), that meaning wasn't very clear that day. But it sure becomes clear now. The lamb conjured up very particular meanings for the Jewish people. First, they would have thought of the lambs that were slaughtered on the day before the first Passover in Egypt and whose blood was spread atop the doorpost of their homes to protect them. This ritual has continued ever since for the Jewish people.

Second, they would have thought of the scapegoat: the animal atop whose head in the Day of Atonement the Jewish high priest would symbolically place the sins of the people during the previous year and then drive it into the wilderness in some hope that God and man could be reconciled again.

But now the Lamb of God becomes clear: The Lamb of God is Jesus. He is the

Passover Lamb that will be slaughtered for us and Whose precious blood will cover not our doors but our hearts. He is the One who takes upon and into Himself all of our sins so that we can become right with God.

Evil quite simply is real. It can't be ignored. It must be addressed.

Pope Benedict has written, "God Himself becomes the place of reconciliation and in the person of His son takes the suffering upon Himself. God Himself grants His infinite purity to the world. God Himself drinks the cup of every horror to the dregs and thereby restores justice through the greatness of His love which through suffering transforms the darkness."[9]

Our Father

Ten Hail Marys

Glory Be

Fatima Prayer

The Fifth Sorrowful Mystery

The Crucifixion and Death
of Our Lord
and Savior Jesus Christ

And Jesus said to fulfill, that is to complete, the Scriptures, *"I thirst"* (John 19:28). In saying this, John means to reveal to us that the Scriptures *in their entirety* have been speaking this one single theme: *God thirsts*. He doesn't thirst for water: He thirsts for *you*. He thirsts for *me*. He thirsts for our faith, for our response to His love revealed once and for all on the Cross in

His total gift of self.

Many years ago, Jesus spoke to St. Mother Teresa about these words. He said, "Have you not understood my cross? Then listen again to the words I spoke there for they tell you clearly why I endured all this for you. I thirst. Yes, I thirst for you. As the rest of the psalm I was praying says of me, I looked for love and I found none. All your life I have been looking for your love. I have never stopped seeking to love you and to be loved by you. You have tried many other things in your search for happiness, why not try opening your heart to me, right now more than you ever have before? For I thirst for you."[10]

Our Father

Ten Hail Marys

Glory Be

Fatima Prayer

Hail Holy Queen

Final Prayer

The Sign of the Cross

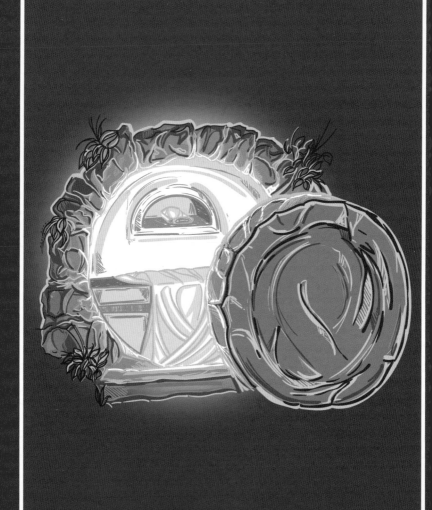

The Glorious Mysteries

"If Christ has not been raised then our preaching is in vain and your faith is in vain," so wrote St. Paul to the Corinthian church (1 Corr. 15:14) way back in the 50s, not the 1950s … the 50s. The heart of our faith is the truth that Jesus of Nazareth, crucified under the Roman procurator Pontius Pilate, is alive, incontestably alive! Not His ideas, not His teachings: He is alive!

A wise teacher of mine often used to say that life on this earth is frequently like one of those massive wall tapestries that became common during the time of the Renaissance. These used to hang in palaces and castles all across Europe. On the front would be a beautiful scene perhaps from Scripture, perhaps of a landscape, maybe some hunters and their dogs out on the prowl. But that beauty was only visible from the front if you were looking at the tapestry.

If you walked behind the tapestry, you didn't see anything beautiful at all. You didn't see anything that made any sense. You just saw a bunch of strings left there by the weavers, hanging down without any apparent rhyme or reason. Our life can often seem that way. Things happen and we not only wonder why but we wonder how anything good can come out of it. That certainly must have been what it seemed like as Jesus was placed in the tomb on Good Friday. It was like looking at the back of the tapestry and nothing made any sense.

But in these Glorious Mysteries, we get a glimpse of the front of the tapestry. We get to see the incredible beauty that has come about at the hands of God the great artist as His Son rises from the dead. And again, we must remember this has happened for you and for me. Because as Christ was raised, so too will we one day be raised.

And though life today might seem like just a bunch of loose threads hanging down to no purpose, one day we will see the beauty that God is weaving out of our lives.

The Sign of the Cross

Apostles' Creed

Our Father
Intention: A prayer for our Holy Father

Three Hail Marys
Intention: For an increase of faith, hope, and charity

Glory Be

The First Glorious Mystery

*The Resurrection of Jesus
from the Dead*

Though the Scriptures are silent about it, it simply must be the case that the first person Jesus appeared to on the day He rose from the dead wasn't Mary Magdalene or Peter but His mother. St. Ignatius and his reflections on the resurrection certainly thought so and so have countless other saints.

Maybe the Scriptures are silent on this because there are simply no words to describe what that scene must have been like when Mary saw the front of the tapestry. When she saw how it all came together. How it was all worth it. How the cross and the tomb and the scourging and the crown of thorns were not the end. Imagine the look on Jesus' face as He showed Himself risen to His mother. Imagine the look on her face as she saw Him alive in glory.

So let us use our imaginations and ask the Holy Spirit to take us to that moment, to see that encounter, to be filled right now with great hope that whatever is taking place in our lives, it's not the last word. The whole world, most especially your life and mine, is truly in His hands.

Our Father

Ten Hail Marys

Glory Be

Fatima Prayer

The Second Glorious Mystery

The Ascension of Jesus into Heaven

On the Feast of the Ascension, we sing at Mass the refrain "God mounts His throne to shouts of joy, a blare of trumpets for the Lord."

Perhaps because my father was a veteran of World War II, the best visual for this event for me has always been the homecoming that he and the other troops experienced when they finally came home after that horrific war.

The real war has been fought and the victory is taking place. Death is vanquished. Hell is overthrown. The devil's power is destroyed more surely than Hitler's or Stalin's.

Jesus now returns into heaven with a human body, joyfully displaying before the angels' gaze the wounds He suffered in His body for you, for me.

But as we contemplate this event, it's important to know that Christ hasn't left us. "I'm with you always," He promised, "until the end of the world" (cf. Matt.

28:20). We are not orphans. Because of His resurrection, Jesus is able to be present now in an entirely new way. His body, though very real, is no longer bound by time and space like ours. He's truly with us. He's especially with us, of course, in the Scriptures that we read, in the Assembly of the faithful gathered together, and, above all, in the Eucharist where He is truly present.

Our Father

Ten Hail Marys

Glory Be

Fatima Prayer

The Third Glorious Mystery

The Descent of the Holy Spirit
on Our Lady and the Apostles
on the Day of Pentecost

The Holy Spirit is in you like heat is in hot water. That is to say . . . everywhere, that's how a man I know puts it. Or as St. Paul puts it, "we are temples of the Holy Spirit" (cf. 1 Cor. 6:19). The spirit within us helps us to understand what Jesus has done for us on the Cross. He moves us to repent, to turn away from our sin in response to what has been done for us. And, He enables us to become entirely new creatures in the waters of Baptism. He helps us to know and to love the Father. He teaches us to pray, for often quite frankly we don't know how to pray as we ought. And, He sends us out into this world to tell others of what God has done for us in Jesus.

Our Father

Ten Hail Marys

Glory Be

Fatima Prayer

The Fourth Glorious Mystery

The Assumption of Our Lady,
Body and Soul into Heaven

Though this dogma of the Church wasn't formally defined until 1950, it's not at all as though it was invented at that time. The Church had held from the earliest days that Mary, as the one who had cooperated most fully in the work of her son either before she died or immediately after she died, had been taken up to heaven to share in His glory. In this, she was showing us our end, that God has made us all to enjoy and experience the infinite joy that is heaven and that joy will be experienced bodily.

Pope Pius XII, together with consultation from the faithful all over the world, defined this dogma formerly in 1950 in part because of the outrages against the human body that had just taken place in World War II. It was important then to remind the world that the destiny of the human person was not a concentration camp or a gulag or a crematorium; the destiny of the human person, every human person, is to be divinized. Our age also needs to be reminded of this with the various assaults against the human person in abortion, poverty, pornography, war, and so many other outrages.

Once again, we are reminded in this Mystery that there are no ordinary people. After the Blessed Sacrament, the holiest object ever presented to our senses is another human being.

Holy Mary, Mother of God help us to know this and to live this.

Our Father

Ten Hail Marys

Glory Be

Fatima Prayer

"THE ONE WHO OVERCOMES, I WILL GRANT HIM TO SIT WITH ME ON MY THRONE, AS I ALSO OVERCAME AND SAT WITH MY FATHER ON HIS THRONE" (REV. 3:21).

The Fifth Glorious Mystery
Crowning of Our Lady as Queen of Heaven and Earth

As we gaze upon Our Lady crowned, to be sure we gaze at the one who perfectly surrendered herself to God, who died daily so as to live entirely for Him, and thus is uniquely able to teach us about the Christian life. But even more than we gaze at the one being crowned, we gaze and worship the One who is placing the crown on Mary's head. We gaze at and worship

135

Jesus. Here, too, it's worth recalling that in Baptism we all became sharers in Christ's Kingship and remember that a true king is not someone who was waited upon but someone who waits on others. "The Son of man came," Jesus said, "not to be served but to serve, and to give his life as a ransom for many" (Matt. 20:28).

Mary uniquely cooperated in this grace. And, we too are called, each in our own way, to give our lives for one another starting with those nearest to us: our wife, our husband, our children, our parents, our siblings, our co-workers, and especially those most in need where Jesus is always hiding in His distressing disguise.

Mary, pray for us that we too may learn the nobility of serving.

Our Father

Ten Hail Marys

Glory Be

Fatima Prayer

Hail Holy Queen

Final Prayer

The Sign of the Cross

The Luminous Mysteries

As most of us know, these quite simply did not exist as part of the Rosary before 2002 when John Paul II added them to the Joyful, Sorrowful, and Glorious Mysteries. His rationale for doing so was simple: if the Rosary is to be a true compendium of the gospel, if the Rosary is to help us better reflect on and to know the Scriptures, well then there was a lot missing. It was fitting to add further events from Jesus' life that focused on some of the most significant moments of His public life.

Luminous has to do with light. Jesus is the light of the world. In other words, because He is both true God and true man, He is uniquely able to reveal to us both who God really is and who we really are as human beings. Pope John Paul II repeated over and over again that only in the light of Christ does the Mystery of the human person become clear. In other words, if I really want to know how to live, I simply must know Jesus because He's the only One who can teach me that authentically.

As we pray with these Mysteries, let's ask

Mary to teach us how to be truly human as we ponder her son.

The Sign of the Cross

Apostles' Creed

Our Father
Intention: A prayer for our Holy Father

Three Hail Marys
Intention: For an increase of faith, hope, and charity

Glory Be

The First Luminous Mystery
The Baptism of Our Lord Jesus

As we know, whenever it rains water rushes to the lowest place, which unfortunately sometimes is our basement. This simple observation can help us understand what's happening in this event. For just as water acts that way, so mercy rushes to the one who is most in need. This is symbolized in the fact that Jesus is baptized in a river, the Jordan, which flows into the lowest place on the face of the earth, the Dead Sea.

As soon as Jesus comes up out of the waters of that river the Spirit of God descends in the form of a dove. Why a dove? Well, one of the early saints put it this way: just as long ago a dove announced to Noah that the flood was over and he and the animals and his family could finally leave the ark, so now the Spirit announces in the form of a dove that the shipwreck of humanity is at an end.[11]

Our Father

Ten Hail Marys

Glory Be

Fatima Prayer

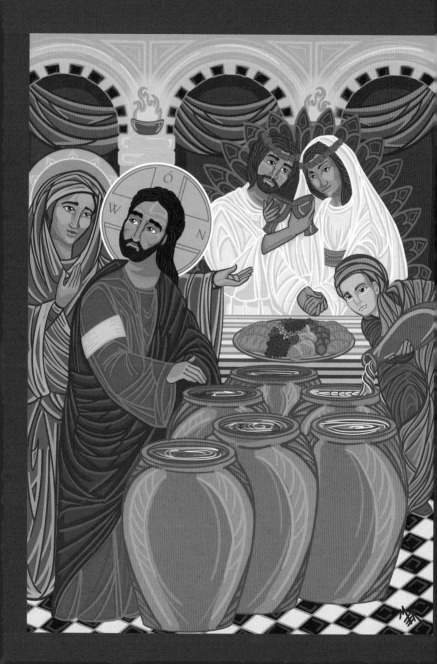

The Second Luminous Mystery
The Wedding Feast at Cana

Jesus chooses as the setting for His first miracle a wedding. Immediately, we might want to pray in a special way for marriages. The miracle, as I'm sure we all know, consisted of changing one hundred and eighty gallons of water into wine. Now to state the obvious, that's a lot of wine!

I once heard a man comment that while

water is a symbol of sustenance, wine is nothing of the kind: Wine is a symbol of joy. The psalmist sings, "you bring forth wine to cheer man's heart" (cf. Psa. 104:14).

It's important here to note that Jesus will not turn bread and *water* into Himself but bread and *wine* into His Body and Blood.

God, and this must be repeated more and more in our present age, is not some kind of celestial killjoy. God is the infinitely joyful, the abundantly happy One.

"I have come," Jesus said, "that you might have life and have it abundantly" (cf. John 10:10). True joy and fullness of life only come from knowing and following Jesus.

Our Father

Ten Hail Marys

Glory Be

Fatima Prayer

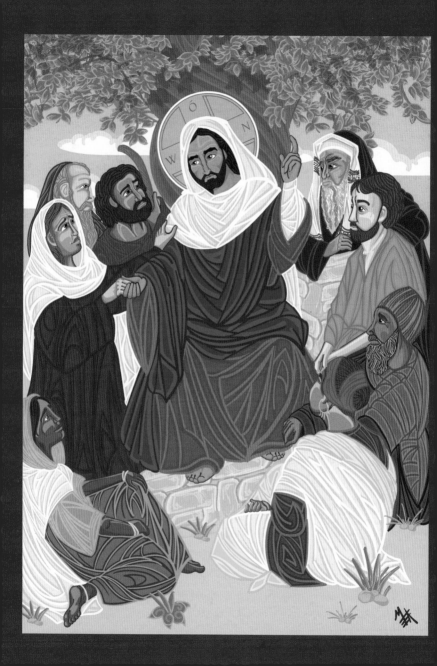

The Third Luminous Mystery
The Preaching of the Gospel

What does "gospel" mean? We hear the word all the time but it's worth asking what it means. It means good news. But what exactly is *the* good news?

One author has put it this way: The gospel, that is the good news, is the proclamation that you by name are far, far, *far* more important than you ever dared to imagine.

For you have been created by God in His own image and likeness. You have been made for eternal friendship with Him, and to enable this to happen *for you,* God has become a man. *For you,* He has suffered. *For you,* He has died. And *for you,* He has been raised. Just for you and for us all. Which means that every time I see another human being I need to remember that that person is no mere mortal: they were made to be divinized. There simply are no ordinary people.

Our Father

Ten Hail Marys

Glory Be

Fatima Prayer

The Fourth Luminous Mystery

*The Transfiguration
of Our Lord Jesus*

"This is My beloved Son; listen to him"
(Mark 9:7).

These words are spoken by God the Father
to Peter, James, and John at the occasion
of Jesus' Transfiguration. At that moment
for the only time before His glorious
Resurrection, Jesus' divinity shone forth
from His body. But we might ask, which

words of Jesus is the Father referring to?

Well, perhaps especially the words spoken just before this scene in the gospel. Words about His Cross, words about how if you and I are going to say yes to His invitation to follow Him, it means that we, too, must take up our cross. This can be and is hard. It lends itself easily to discouragement. The Christian life is no casual stroll in the park. It will be and it is arduous.

Much like a coach reminding his players of the goal they're training so hard for, so Jesus after speaking about the Cross lets the three apostles, and now us, get a glimpse of the goal, a glimpse of what comes after the Cross—His Cross and your cross. And what comes after the Cross is life and glory and joy.

Our Father

Ten Hail Marys

Glory Be

Fatima Prayer

The Fifth Luminous Mystery
The Institution of the Eucharist

It is simply an indisputable historical fact that from the very beginning Jesus' followers understood the Eucharist not to be a mere symbol but truly His Body and Blood hidden under the appearance of bread and wine.

Perhaps we would do well here to ask ourselves why. Why does Jesus give us

Himself in the Eucharist? Do you and I ever stop to think that at the end of that long Communion line at Mass is not merely some priest or extraordinary minister of the Eucharist but really the Lord Himself standing, giving Himself to us?

Maybe the answer is as simple as this: because God is love and what love wants, what love really wants, is union. But now in being united to Him, we must imitate Him. Meaning what? Meaning we too must break open our lives for one another. Jesus said that it is by our love for each other that all would know we are His disciples (cf. John 13:35).

Our Father

Ten Hail Marys

Glory Be

Fatima Prayer

Hail Holy Queen

Final Prayer

The Sign of the Cross

Resources

1. *Vatican,* "Apostolic Journey to Poland: Holy Mass and Act of Consecration to the Mother of God, **Homily of His Holiness John Paul II**, Czetochowa-Jasna Gora, 4 June 1979," http://www.vatican.va/content/john-paul-ii/en/homilies/1979/documents/hf_jp-ii_hom_19790604_polonia-jasna-gora.html.

2. *Archives du Carmel de Lisieux,* "LT 261- to Fr. Bellière – July 26, 1897," http://www.archives-carmel-lisieux.fr/english/carmel/index.php/lt-261-a-266/1172-lt-261-a-labbe-belliere.

3. St. Thérèse, *The Story of a Soul: The Autobiography of St. Thérèse of Lisieux.* Charlotte, NC: Tan Books, 2010.

4. *Vatican,* "Apostolic Letter: ***Rosarium Virginis Mariae*** of the Supreme Pontiff John Paul II to the Bishops, Clergy, and Faithful on the Most Holy Rosary," http://www.vatican.va/content/john-paul-ii/en/apost_letters/2002/documents/hf_jp-ii_apl_20021016_rosarium-virginis-mariae.html.

5. *Vatican,* "***Supremi Apostolatus Officio*** Encyclical of Pope Leo XIII on Devotion of the Rosary," https://www.vatican.va/content/leo-xiii/en/encyclicals/documents/hf_l-xiii_enc_01091883_supremi-apostolatus-officio.html.

6. *Vatican,* "Apostolic Letter: ***Rosarium Virginis Mariae*** of the Supreme Pontiff John Paul II to the Bishops, Clergy, and Faithful on the Most Holy Rosary," https://www.vatican.va/content/john-paul-ii/en/apost_letters/2002/documents/hf_jp-ii_apl_20021016_rosarium-virginis-mariae.html.

7. *Vatican,* "***Radio Message of His Holiness Pius XII to Participants in the National Catechetical Congress of the United States in Boston,*** Pontifical Palace in Castel Gandolfo, Saturday, 26 October 1946," http://www.vatican.va/content/pius-xii/en/speeches/1946/documents/hf_p-xii_spe_19461026_congresso-catechistico-naz.html.

8. Joseph Ratzinger, [Pope Benedict XVI]. *Jesus of Nazareth: Part Two, Holy Week from the Entrance into Jerusalem to the Resurrection.*
San Francisco, CA: Ignatius Press, 2011.

9. Ibid.

10. Catholic Link, "'*I Thirst for You*'–A Letter from Mother Teresa." http://catholic-link.org/quotes/i-thirst-letter-written-mother-teresa-quote/.

11. St. Peter Chrysologus, Sermon 160.

AUTHOR

Fr. John Riccardo was ordained a priest of the Archdiocese of Detroit in 1996, where he served as a pastor for 15 years. He is the Founder and Executive Director of ACTS XXIX, a non-profit apostolate that exists because God wants His world back. ACTS XXIX equips clergy and lay leaders for the apostolic age in which we live. He is the host of the radio program *Christ is the Answer* and the podcast *You Were Born For This with Fr. John Riccardo*. His most recent book *Rescued: The Unexpected and Extraordinary News of the Gospel* is available at www.wau.org. To learn more about ACTS XXIX, please visit www.actsxxix.org.

ILLUSTRATOR

Marie Mattos is an illustrator, graphic designer, and artist living in Metro Detroit, Michigan, with her husband and two little boys. As a graduate of Michigan State University, her favorite media to work in are acrylics on wood panel and digital painting. Her style is a marriage of Christian iconography and vibrant tattoo art. Falling in love with drawing at an early age, Marie believes creating art is an act of worship, and her greatest desire is to attract hearts of all ages into a personal encounter with Jesus through her illustrations. You can view more of her work at mariemattos.com.